LITERARY

A Celebration of Magical Women Writers

WITCHES

TAISIA KITAISKAIA

ILLUSTRATED BY
Katy Horan

SEAL

TO THE CREATIVE WOMEN IN OUR LIVES

Seal Press
Hachette Book Group
1290 Avenue of the Americas, New York, NY 10104
sealpress.com
@SealPress
Printed in Canada

First Edition: October 2017

.Published by Seal Press, an imprint of Perseus Books, LLC,
a subsidiary of Hachette Book Group, Inc.

The publisher is not responsible for websites (or their content)
that are not owned by the publisher.

Selected images with accompanying text first published
in Electric Literature's Okey-Panky

Cover and print book interior design by Kimberly Glyder

Library of Congress Control Number: 2017951205

ISBNs: 978-1-58005-673-1 (hardcover), 978-1-58005-674-8 (ebook)

FRI

10   9   8   7   6   5   4

TABLE OF CONTENTS

PREFACE

Because all artists are magicians, and Witches wield a special magic. Witches and women writers alike dwell in creativity, mystery, and other worlds. They aren't afraid to be alone in the woods of their imaginations, or to live in huts of their own making. They're not afraid of the dark.

As such, the mantle of "Literary Witch" is the highest honor we can bestow upon an author. The thirty writers included here inspire us deeply, urging us to be creatively courageous. We've crafted their portraits in art and writing to pay homage to their presences, and to access their spirits through our own mediums.

Due to time, space, and seniority (long-practicing Witches must be noted before newly initiated Witches), the authors that follow make up only a single shelf of our role-model library. We hope that you will celebrate them with us, read their works, and go out to create your own canon of Literary Witches.

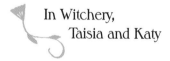

In Witchery,
Taisia and Katy

FOREWORD
by Pam Grossman

as an insult, an identifier, a badge of honor. We picture a witch, and we picture a multiplicity: She's a hideous woman in a pointed hat. A sibyl swaying with prophetic visions. A bride of the devil. A devotee to the divine feminine. A Salem villager. An herbalist. A seductress. A forest dweller in a hut made of detritus or chicken legs or candy. A 1990s teenager in pentagrams and plaid. What does the word *witch* mean, though? And perhaps more importantly: what do we mean when we use it?

The origin is unclear. A bit of research will tell you that it's perhaps a derivation of Old Germanic words that mean "wise" or "to bend" or "willow." I like all these options, even more so when considered together. I think of someone who is knowledgeable in the art of shape-shifting. Someone plugged into an ancient current. Someone who is pliable not out of resignation but out of self-preservation. She's an intelligent, resilient being who changes with the times, and changes the times along with her. One thing is certain: a witch is almost always a "she." And I've come to realize that the Witch is arguably the only female archetype that has power on its own terms. She is not defined by anyone else. Wife, sister, mother, virgin, whore—these archetypes draw meaning based on relationships with others. The Witch, however, is a woman who stands entirely on her own. She is more often than not an outsider, and her gift is transformation. She is a change agent, and her work is sparked by speech: an incantation, a naming, a blessing, a curse.

Who is more worthy of this moniker than female writers, who themselves conjure worlds out of words? Certainly they have much in common with witches: women who create things other than children are still considered dangerous by many. They are marginalized, trivialized, or totally ignored. Too often they are excluded from the artistic canon—but they are weaponized nonetheless.

For let's recall that many occultic words are connected to those of language: *Spelling* and *spells*. *Grammar* and *grimoire*. *Abracadabra* is thought to be derived from an Aramaic phrase that translates to "I create like the word." To write, then, is to make magic. And so it follows that to be a female writer is, in fact, to be a kind of Witch.

This book in your hands also contains multitudes. It is a course corrective, an inspiration potion, a mystic dossier. Reading *Literary Witches* is like climbing through a feminist family tree, with gnarled roots, fruit-laden branches, and leaves of letters that offer sustenance and shelter.

Through this luminous volume, we trace a legacy of language, connected by gender if not genetics. It positions these writers as members of a coven: one in which Mirabai, Mary Shelley, Octavia Butler, and María Sabina each has her moment in the center of the circle. And we, the reader, are allowed entrance as well. Our offering is our attention to each bright life we encounter here.

Taisia Kitaiskaia supplies us with the *hexen* text. Her three "facts" about each Witch writer read like surrealist invocations. She weaves morsels of their biographies with her own channeled visions. Odd and lovely images surface in her scrying glass. She mixes the "factual" with the "true" in her brew, and elevates each woman to the realm of legend.

She writes that Virginia Woolf "leaps easily from one pool of consciousness to another," and so we think simultaneously of Mrs. Dalloway and a High Priestess in trance.

We're told of Audre Lorde that "in night's secret wood, where women go to eat their own hearts, Audre is a goddess rising from a pond of lava." I, for one, can attest that Lorde's writings make me glow with inner fire, and that I have worshipped at her altar on many a dark occasion.

About Anne Carson, Kitaiskaia writes, "Sappho, Sokrates, and Sophokles are a few of the ghosts that haunt Anne's nights." Whether this should be read as an allusion to Carson's classicist streak or as evidence of necromancy is uncertain. After all, who's to say that Carson doesn't convene with phantoms in the evenings? Far be it from me.

Therein lies the immense pleasure of this book. As readers, we're pulled between a desire to decipher these fragments and an eagerness to surrender to their delicious mystery.

Katy Horan's strange and tender illustrations capture this spirit perfectly. A painter who specializes in folkloric scenes of feminine magic, she has found ideal subject matter here. Each of her portraits is reminiscent of religious iconography, embellished with miraculous elements and secret symbols throughout. No stranger to Witches, she is perhaps best known for her paintings of crones and naked ladies who engage in woodland rituals and make talismans from string and lace.

Weavers, potters, cooks, and healers—all have Witchly connotations, for they have traditionally been women with the gift of alchemizing something crude into something fine. For Horan to include female writers in her ongoing visual narrative makes perfect sense. By painting them, she elevates them from the chthonic to the celestial. Each of these illustrations is its own self-contained constellation, glittering with beauty and charm.

Taken together, Kitaiskaia's words and Horan's pictures form one grand working. *Literary Witches* is their shared spell for feminine crafting that raises the dead, honors the ancestors, and takes us to a place where women have full creative sovereignty.

It is a curious compendium to be sure. Read it, and you will assuredly be drawn to further tomes and poems. You may even become enchanted enough to write something new yourself.

As to how to approach this book? There is no set order imposed. I suggest you begin oracularly: pick a section at random, in an act of bibliomancy. It will lead you to someone wise and wonderful and wildly free, no doubt.

Go ahead. Flip to any page. Follow your wyrd.

Welcome the Witch.

EMILY BRONTË

RECLUSIVE BRITISH NOVELIST

1818-1848

WATCHER OF THE MOORS, FANTASY, AND CRUEL ROMANCE

WHEN SHE BRUSHES the carpet, Emily imagines she is smoothing the moors for Heathcliff's perfect feet. He'll come in, Emily dreams, like the winds she walks against—muscular gusts, clenched hands snarling under her coats.

WHAT DO THE ants whisper to Emily as they climb the ruined trees outside? She puts her ear to the bark and listens. She will join their palace . . . She will be their ant queen . . . She will pit them against other ant queendoms. . . . She will watch their love and war play out.

EMILY MAKES A telescope from ice and twine. Through this tunnel, she stares into her own eye until she sees a galaxy, and through the galaxy until she sees a stranger's eye.

Emily Brontë spent her uneventful life at the family home on the moors. She created fantasy worlds with her brilliant sisters (Charlotte and Anne), brushed the carpet, and took walks in the hills. She achieved posthumous fame for *Wuthering Heights*, a vicious novel of romance between two isolated, stormy characters—Catherine and Heathcliff—after her death of tuberculosis at thirty.

RECOMMENDED READING

Novel of Brutal Love: *Wuthering Heights*

Poetry of the Brontë Coven: *Poems by Currer, Ellis, and Acton Bell*

Best Writing About Emily: "The Glass Essay," by (fellow Witch) Anne Carson

OCTAVIA
BUTLER

SCIENCE FICTION WRITER

1947-2006

SOWER OF STRANGE SEEDS, SPECIES, AND THE FUTURE

OCTAVIA TAKES A break from writing to water her plants. The potted heads, of various races and humanoid species, totter on thick stems and wave their leaves at her as she enters the greenhouse. She feeds them from her pitcher.

BUYING GROCERIES, OCTAVIA looks around at the people putting cabbages and apples into their carts, and sees what will one day overtake the innocent scene: communities overpopulating, mutating with violent need for food, power, and sex.

WALKING BACK FROM the store, Octavia covertly tosses the seeds she always keeps in her pockets into her neighbors' yards. Seeds that won't save us but urge, *We can do better.*

Octavia E. Butler, the daughter of a housekeeper and a shoeshiner, was a pioneer in the very white- and male-dominated genre of science fiction. She received a MacArthur "Genius" Grant for her dark, philosophical novels and stories, which feature black female protagonists and explore power dynamics between sexes, races, and species.

RECOMMENDED READING

Time-Travelling Slave Narrative: *Kindred*

Novel Starring an Immortal, Shape-Shifting African Woman: *Wild Seed*

Violent, Thought-Provoking Stories: *Bloodchild and Other Stories*

SHIRLEY JACKSON

AMERICAN HORROR WRITER

1916-1965

WITCH OF VILLAGES, DOMESTIC HORRORS, AND OMENS

TO ESCAPE HER demonic children, Shirley once had a long, antagonistic argument with her hair dryer in the bathroom. Won.

WHILE STILL ALIVE, Shirley transformed the stones neighbors threw at her into rabid cats, poisoned beetles, blood-tipped needles. She buried these treasures in the backyard. Years later, the treasures crawl back up through the soil. The neighborhood is plagued by pests and pins to this day.

SHIRLEY'S GHOST HAUNTS the ice cream section of your twenty-four-hour grocery store at three a.m., wearing cotton socks and noting human behavior on a little writing pad. She doesn't need help finding anything.

Shirley Jackson's fiction, which marries the ordinary with the supernatural, often speaks to the inhumanities people are prone to when given half a chance. Her most famous story on the subject, "The Lottery," was written after rural Vermont residents painted a swastika on her house (her husband, a professor at Bennington College, was Jewish). Yet keen observation and a sense of humor pervade many of her works, especially her very funny essays on raising four kids.

RECOMMENDED READING

Unforgettable Tale: "The Lottery"

Delightfully Wicked Novel: *We Have Always Lived in the Castle*

Creepiest: *The Haunting of Hill House*

Comic Essays on Family Life: *Life Among the Savages; Raising Demons*

EILEEN CHANG

GIANT OF MODERN CHINESE LITERATURE

1920-1995

ENCHANTRESS OF BITTER LOVE, TREACHERY, AND JEWELS

EILEEN CRAFTS A spell to escape the claustrophobia of family and custom. She summons a moonbeam into her locked room; a trapdoor materializes in the light. She climbs down . . .

. . . BUT ALL SHE finds is an underground chamber. Eileen hears her lover calling to her in the dark, but she can't seem to reach him. Voices echoing, the lovers never find each other . . .

. . . SO EILEEN PULLS herself up by the moonbeam still pouring through the trapdoor. Back in her room, with nowhere left to go, she puts on a gorgeous gown with pearl buttons, slips on a jade bracelet. She stares into the mirror, watching her mind turn sumptuous as silk. She announces: "I am the ruler of this prison." The moon stays at her side until morning.

Eileen Chang was born to an opium-addicted, traditional father and a Westernized mother who learned to ski on bound feet. When seventeen-year-old Chang contracted dysentery, her father and his concubine dismissed her claims of ill health and locked her up in her bedroom for six months; she escaped with the help of her nurse. Witty and stylish, Chang was famous in Japanese-occupied Shanghai for her fiction about troubled romance and family betrayal. Though she died as a recluse in Los Angeles, her work remains popular and beloved in China and has been adapted into films by directors such as Ang Lee.

RECOMMENDED READING

Heartbreaking Love Story: *Half a Lifelong Romance*

Famous, Film-Adapted Works: *Love in a Fallen City*; *Red Rose, White Rose*; *Lust, Caution*

Novels Written in English: *Naked Earth, The Rice-Sprout Song*

SYLVIA PLATH

ICONIC CONFESSIONAL POET

1932–1963

FURY OF MOTHERHOOD, MARRIAGE, AND THE MOON

THREE SYLVIA HOLOGRAMS SURVIVE THE ORIGINAL SYLVIA:

THE FIRST DISMEMBERS male mannequins with ferocious, precise claws. Bees spill from the hollow arms and legs. The bees swarm on to enact Sylvia's revenge.

THE SECOND SYLVIA rules a small, cold planet with no other inhabitants. She sips a mysterious liquid from an ornate bowl, watches the mothers on Earth making breakfast for their children, and laughs.

THE THIRD SYLVIA is a shiny black disc, dragging itself from yew to elm, bed to oven. Everything the disc passes, hearing that black crackle, is terrified into the thrill of living.

Born in Boston, Sylvia Plath was a social and academic success in spite of intense depressions and suicide attempts. On a Fulbright scholarship to Cambridge University, she met and married the poet Ted Hughes. While Hughes philandered and kept bees, Plath stayed at home with two young children and wrote increasingly brilliant, scary poetry that made use of her anger at husband and father, intense mental states, and obsession with death. At thirty, Plath ended her life by putting her head in the oven.

RECOMMENDED READING

The Masterpiece: *Ariel*

Classics: "Lady Lazarus," "Daddy," "Cut"

More Classics: "The Applicant," "Edge," "Tulips"

TONI
MORRISON

NOBEL PRIZE-WINNING NOVELIST

B. 1931

QUEEN OF MIRACLES, GENERATIONS, AND MEMORY

QUEEN TONI SEES — cleaving from the skin of every person—the child they were, their parents, great-grandparents, all the way to the first human. She can see this ancestor's original hurt, carried around in the generations like a splinter in the spleen.

WITH HER MIND, Toni ferries her people's unsettled ghosts across hostile rivers, carves smooth blue boats for them to travel in. Builds shelters to cradle their rest before the great migration.

TONI IS AT velvet ease at her throne. Her supplicants line up to present offerings of rubies, roast duck, wildflowers. But one approaches empty handed: he tells Toni a joke instead. Everyone gasps. Finally, Toni lets out a big, rumbling laugh and joy flushes through the palace.

No American writer is more honor-laden than regal Toni Morrison, who was born to a working-class family in Lorain, Ohio—a frequent setting for her epic novels of black experience. Her most famous work, *Beloved*, has become required reading, but wave that unjust homework aura away. Seek it for the haunted story it is, a deeply spooky and moving book about a vengeful baby ghost.

RECOMMENDED READING

Most Magical: *Beloved*

Novels for the Ages: *Song of Solomon, Sula*

Banned Book: *The Bluest Eye*

ANNA AKHMATOVA

GREAT RUSSIAN POET

1889-1966

KOLDUNYA OF WINTER, ENDURANCE, AND WILLOWS

AFTER STALIN THREATENS her family, Anna fires up the cauldron: in go the ripped pages of forbidden manuscripts. The sodden papers become bandages for the wounded. The bitter broth—gulped down, so the words are never forgotten.

THE DEATHS OF Anna's people are woven into her shawl. She sucks on these silver threads during the famine to stay alive.

ANNA WAITS IN line for rations of potatoes, cabbage, and milk. When it's her turn, the government official slips Anna a strange object. "You must tell our story," she says. Anna looks down and sees a golden egg. She can hear the wild heart of her nation beating inside.

Anna Akhmatova was celebrated during and beyond her lifetime for her lyric, melancholy poetry. As Russia fell under Stalin, Akhmatova and her circle of artists and intellectuals were persecuted for their work: her son was imprisoned and sent to labor camps and her husband was executed. Akhmatova's most famous poem, "Requiem," is her boldest attempt at capturing the Stalinist terror.

RECOMMENDED READING

Lovely Selected: *Poems of Akhmatova*, trans. Stanley Kunitz

Epic Masterpiece: "Requiem"

Lyric Beauties: "Willow," "Lot's Wife," "The Last Toast"

JOY HARJO

MVSKOKE POET AND MUSICIAN

B. 1951

ALL THE ELEMENTS are at Joy's command: fire and water fighting in her belly, earth listening for her feet's instructions, wind whipping up a storm inside her mouth.

JOY LIES DOWN in a field and closes her eyes. Hooves rumble towards her. Soon, the horses are upon her, snorting, nuzzling her hair, crunching on her apple offerings. As always, when she opens her eyes, nothing is there.

A STRANGE MUSIC hums in and outside of Joy. She follows the sound. Doesn't stop when the music takes her all the way to the sun. The music is a spell, protecting Joy from the heat of the sun and the heat of the great star within her own chest.

Harjo, a common Mvskoke (Creek) Nation name, means "so brave she's crazy." Joy Harjo courageously survived an oppressive childhood, teenage pregnancy, and domestic abuse before becoming a spiritually charged poet of wild natural imagery and urgent social activism, as well as an award-winning saxophone player and singer.

RECOMMENDED READING

Most Bewitching: "She Had Some Horses"

Essential Poetry: *How We Became Human*

Painful, Inspiring Memoir: *Crazy Brave*

FLANNERY O'CONNOR

AUTHOR OF SOUTHERN GOTHIC FICTION

1925-1964

SEER OF PEACOCKS, WEIRD COUNTRY PEOPLE, AND GLASS EYES

FLANNERY PRAYS TO see humanity clearly. She rests her head on her desk. Blood drains out her ear and spreads into a pool. Little figures— a woman with a wooden leg, a grandma wearing an awful hat, and a ratty, sinister youth—wobble across the pool on tiny, dirty ice skates.

ON HER DEATHBED, Flannery learns the language of chickens. She squawks a song irresistible to her peacocks, and dozens fly in through the window. The peacocks serenade her with their tails, amuse her with petty talk. When Flannery loses all her hair, they bite off their own feathers to crown her with a headdress.

FLANNERY'S MIND CONTINUES to rumble through the hills. When your car breaks down in the middle of Georgia, a dusty bus with no driver or passengers pulls in from the heat. You hear a woman's voice on the intercom: "Next stop, a serial killer confronts a cabbage-faced family." The doors creak open. You don't know whether to run, or join the spectacle.

Flannery O'Connor wrote cutting, hilarious, and (secretly, devoutly) Catholic stories about the Deep South. Growing up in Georgia, O'Connor loved chickens and knit coats for her fowl. After graduating from the Iowa Writers' Workshop and hitting her stride in fiction, she contracted lupus and moved back in with her mother. She populated their farm with more than forty peacocks.

RECOMMENDED READING

The Gritty Hits: "A Good Man Is Hard to Find," "Good Country People,"
    "Everything That Rises Must Converge" (*The Complete Stories*)

Best-Loved Novel: *Wise Blood*

Fantastic Essay About Raising Peacocks: "The King of the Birds"

SAPPHO

LYRIC POET OF ANCIENT GREECE

630-570 BCE

SIREN OF THE LYRE, HONEY, AND RUINS

SAPPHO IS THE hot green insect in every jealous quarrel, zinging between you and your lover, agitating the ions, biting your skin and making you seethe, raising the hair on the cat's back.

SAPPHO IS THE beautiful woman you lock eyes with across the party. She has a garland and a sweet voice, and no matter how many times you try to get closer, she eludes you. Finally, she approaches, only to push a piece of papyrus into your hands and slip out the door. All you can make out is *you burning* in perfect handwriting. The rest of the words are illegible.

SAPPHO IS A pair of wings—pearling between pigeon blue, moody emerald, and golden white—smoldering in a hidden cave. The wings disappear from time to time, reappearing in young girls' closets. How seriously each girl puts these wings on in the mirror, readying herself for the pain and pleasure of love.

Before Plato and Homer, there was Sappho, literary star of ancient Greece and the first female homoerotic poet. Plato called her the "Tenth Muse," and her reputation has survived to this day. However, her sung and lyre-accompanied poetry—of bittersweet love between women—has been lost to time, fire, and religious disapproval. Only a few fragments remain.

RECOMMENDED READING

Best Translation: *If Not, Winter*, trans. Anne Carson (fellow Witch)

Single Complete Poem: "Deathless Aphrodite of the spangled mind"

Most Striking Fragment: "He seems to me equal to gods that man . . . "

FORUGH
FARROKHZAD

ICONOCLASTIC IRANIAN POET AND FILMMAKER

1935-1967

REBEL OF SENSUAL LOVE, GREEN GARDENS, AND PERFUME

TIRED OF BEING a woman, Forugh turns into an acacia tree. Stars in her branches and fish in the pond at her feet, she waits for her lover to come. At last, the wind arrives. . . . He blows around her limbs, embracing. The acacia's veins flood with wine. But the wind doesn't stay for long. He moves on through the lonely field, and the wine in Forugh's veins brims with agony.

WORKERS IN THE field, disturbed by the acacia's female form—are those breasts in the bark?—chop the tree down. When the tree falls, the men see a woman's naked spirit rise from the acacia. They never speak of it, but each man is haunted by his vision.

NOW THE SPIRIT of the acacia visits dying gardens throughout Iran. She goes wherever there is parched land or neglected flower beds. She floats over withered leaves, wilted geraniums and lilacs. Listening to her songs of love, the roots tingle, the buds swell. Fish return to the ponds, and the trees sway, a strange drunkenness in their sap.

Forugh Farrokhzad's sensual, nature-rich poetry places her among Iran's greatest poets. Heavily criticized for resisting societal norms, Farrokhzad divorced at twenty-one years old, embarked on passionate affairs, was the first Persian poet to write explicitly about sexuality, worked as a documentary filmmaker (check out the award-winning *The House Is Black*), and adopted a son from a leper colony. Some believe that she prophesied her accidental early death in a car crash in the poem "Let Us Believe in the Beginning of the Cold Season."

RECOMMENDED READING

Best Translation: *Sin: Selected Poems of Forugh Farrokhzad*, trans. Sholeh Wolpé

Early Rebellious Poems: "The Captive," "The Ring," "Sin"

Mature Gems: "Reborn," "Wind-Up Doll," "I Pity the Garden"

EMILY DICKINSON

ONE OF THE GREATEST POETS OF ALL TIME

1830-1886

SPECTER OF WINDOWS, FLIES, AND THE UNEXPECTED

EMILY TRAVELS FREELY BETWEEN THE AFTERWORLD AND THIS WORLD.
SOMETIMES, NOSTALGIC, SHE RETURNS. . . .

YOU MIGHT LOOK into your garden and see a white dress kneeling in the flowerbeds. No body in it. That's Emily, come back to Earth to joke with her worm friends.

OR YOU MIGHT notice a comely mink in the Amherst woods, whispering to a pond. Every year, Emily possesses this particular mink to recite her new poems, in mink language, to her best reader, the black pond.

BUT YOU ARE luckiest if you see her on a rooftop, wearing flies' wings. Before you can say her name, Emily swoops on from house to house, country to country, observing and perceiving. When she tires, God sends her a ditch, and Emily leaps into it, falling down—and down—

Emily Dickinson spent her whole life in Amherst, Massachusetts. Refusing conventional religion and her prominent family's exhausting social schedule, she instead cultivated a unique spiritual and social life. She wrote long letters to friends, worked in the garden, and created strikingly original poetry about God, death, pain, and love. When Dickinson died, even those closest to her were shocked to find her life's work of eighteen hundred poems neatly folded in a drawer.

RECOMMENDED READING

The Tome: *The Poems of Emily Dickinson* (Reading Edition), ed. R. W. Franklin

The Carry-with-You-Everywhere: *Dickinson: Poems* (Everyman's Library Pocket Poets)

Start Here: "Wild Nights — Wild nights!," "I felt a Funeral, in my Brain," "I dwell in Possibility —," "The Moon is distant from the Sea —," "There's a certain Slant of light," "Fame is a fickle food," "You left me — Sire — two Legacies —," "The World is not Conclusion"

AUDRE LORDE

POET, ESSAYIST, CIVIL RIGHTS ACTIVIST

1934-1992

WARRIOR WITCH OF OTHERNESS, BODIES ELECTRIC, AND SISTERHOOD

DIRECTIONS TO AN Audre Lorde lecture take you to a cave. Audre hands you a torch and a sword at the entrance. The torch is for finding the hieroglyphics inside. The sword is for slaying ghosts and demons along the way. Audre's voice at your back is for pushing you onward.

IN NIGHT'S SECRET wood, where women go to eat their own hearts, Audre is a goddess rising from a pond of lava. Women approach timidly but accept her proffered hand. Audre dips them into the bubbling gold and they emerge in molten suits, lava filling their wounds.

AUDRE'S CORONER WRITES: *Subject's left arm appears to be a dozing woman. Right arm is a little girl drinking milk from her palm. Back is a huddled mother. Legs, two women kissing. Hair is tadpoles. Eyes, snails. Tongue, a frog—* The frog springs onto the coroner's face, and he runs screaming from the room.

Born in NYC to West Indian parents, Audre Lorde proudly proclaimed herself a black lesbian feminist. As an activist and essayist, she was outspoken about racism, sexism, and homophobia. In addition to these themes, her work is populated with mothers, children, sisters, anger, cancer, the erotic, unicorns, snails eating dead snakes, witches, fire, and the importance of refusing silence, period.

RECOMMENDED READING

Witchiest Poems: *The Black Unicorn*

Famous Essays: *Sister Outsider* ("Poetry Is Not a Luxury," "Uses of the Erotic")

Biomythographical Novel: *Zami: A New Spelling of My Name*

ANGELA CARTER

BRITISH AUTHOR OF FICTION AND FAIRY TALES

1940-1992

FAIRY GODMOTHER OF BLOODY TALES, THE CIRCUS, AND MIRRORS

ANGELA STEPS INTO an elevator with a group of businessmen. The doors shut. She sees that one man has the head of a boar. Another— a tiger. A lion. Each clutches his briefcase, ornate rings glinting between hairy knuckles, and stares up at the changing floor numbers.

ANGELA IS WATERING roses when a demure female doll in a red riding habit enters the garden. *Not another one.* Angela rolls her eyes. She takes out her knife and stabs the doll in the heart. The riding habit collapses and a bleeding wolf escapes from under the cloth, dashes out of the garden. Dark drops of blood sink into the soil and Angela's roses bloom a deeper, more delicious red.

WHILE MOURNERS ATTEND Angela's sober funeral, her soul bows glamorously on a grand stage. She holds hands with two elderly, sequined showgirls, and though the audience is empty, the ladies exit to raucous applause.

Angela Carter's feminist fairy tales, which draw on stories like "Little Red Riding Hood" and "Beauty and the Beast," are sumptuous tapestries depicting sexual, violent scenes, ornamented with symbols and adjectives. She was fascinated by the performance of femininity, and her works often feature showgirls, trapeze artists, and dolls.

RECOMMENDED READING

Enchanted Feminist Tales: *The Bloody Chamber*

Burlesque Novels: *Nights at the Circus, Wise Children*

Feminist Nonfiction on Sexual Empowerment: *The Sadeian Woman: And the Ideology of Pornography*

VIRGINIA WOOLF

VISIONARY BRITISH MODERNIST

1882–1941

GUARDIAN OF THE WATERS, THE PORCELAIN, AND THE LEXICON

CROSSING THE STREET on a rainy day, Virginia leaps easily from one pool of consciousness to another. She loves these puddles, the creatures wrapping around her ankles in each. But before she can get to the next street, Virginia sees her own pool: it floods with rain, rises higher, becomes a deep, turbulent river. She will not survive this one.

CARRIED ALONG IN her river, Virginia's body becomes a lighthouse—a tower of perception with one large eye, illuminating all she sees with rich, buttery vision, transforming bottom-feeding fish and debris into objects of beauty and meaning.

BEFORE VIRGINIA IS pulled under forever, a wolf cub leaps from the lighthouse's eye, like Athena from Zeus's forehead. This is Virginia's only child. The wolf daughter fights her way to the bank of the river. She survives.

Virginia Woolf helped usher in a major new literary movement with her stream-of-consciousness fiction, which focuses intensely on the experience of awareness and moves fluidly between the inner lives of its characters. Her personal life (childfree, sexually liberated) and incisive feminist essays were no less radical. After a lifelong struggle with mental illness, Woolf put stones in her pockets and stepped into the river near her Sussex home.

RECOMMENDED READING

Start Here: *Mrs. Dalloway*

Most Exquisite Novel: *To the Lighthouse*

Feminist Nonfiction: *A Room of One's Own*, "Professions for Women"

SANDRA CISNEROS

GROUNDBREAKING MEXICAN-AMERICAN WRITER

B. 1954

HECHICERA DE LOS NOMBRES, LAS CASAS, Y LA SOLEDAD

SANDRA LIVES INSIDE a mango. She writes at her mango desk, eats her way to the mango kitchen. Sometimes the mango is perfectly juicy, sometimes underripe. Sometimes too sweet, or bruised. But it is Sandra's mango, no one else's.

SANDRA RADIATES LIKE la Virgen de Guadalupe, vibrating with all her senses. A cigar in hand, she walks into the jacaranda trees, hanging black lace bras off the branches. Jaguars trail the hem of her holy glow.

WOMEN TRAPPED IN husbands' and fathers' houses wake up with their hair cut off, braided into ropes. *Use this to climb out,* read the notes tied on with ribbon. Out the window, down in the street, Sandra winks and opens her arms.

Born in a working-class Chicago neighborhood to a Mexican father and Mexican-American mother, Sandra Cisneros navigates the richness—and misogyny—of both Hispanic and American cultures. She vowed to never marry and to always have a house of her own. Her most famous book, *The House on Mango Street*, a coming-of-age novel of saturated, sensory vignettes, is taught in elementary schools and colleges alike. Make sure to check out her poetry, too, which asserts a healthy sexuality, and her masterful short stories.

RECOMMENDED READING

Best-Ever Coming-of-Age Novel: *The House on Mango Street*

Sexy Witch Poetry: *Loose Woman*

Subversive Short Stories: *Woman Hollering Creek and Other Stories*

CHARLOTTE PERKINS GILMAN

AMERICAN POWERHOUSE OF FEMINISM,

SOCIALISM, AND FICTION

1860-1935

SOOTHSAYER OF UTOPIAS, CREEPING WOMEN, AND EVIL WALLPAPER

TURN-OF-THE-CENTURY American photographs show an odd pattern: A mother listens to an invisible speaker by the fireplace. A wife, shopping, holds an orange to her ear. Three women gather in the park to stare at nothing—or is that a flicker of light? In each photo, it is Charlotte, the unseen fairy, who holds the women's attention, whispering the changes to come.

THE DAY CHARLOTTE begins her career is the day she notices the drawing-room wallpaper. It looks uncomfortable and itchy, like someone trapped in a wool sweater, so she peels the paper off in big strips. A secret mural is revealed, depicting a land of abundant fruit, clean cities, nourished children, men and women working alongside one another. The wall exhales a sigh of relief.

CHARLOTTE LEARNS EARLY on that she has magic powers. She has only to wave her wand and societies will right themselves, all will be as she envisions. But she tucks the wand away in her pocket and practices an upcoming speech instead. The people must realize the changes for themselves.

Charlotte Perkins Gilman is best known for "The Yellow Wall-Paper," a story inspired by the disastrous, sexist "rest cure" prescribed for her postpartum depression. In her day, Gilman was also famous as a social critic, giving popular lectures on economic and social reform, and for her unconventional life choices. Her utopian novels and nonfiction are worth revisiting for their visions of a cooperative society and the place of gender roles in economics.

RECOMMENDED READING

Essential Tales: "The Yellow Wall-Paper," "When I Was a Witch"

Best of the Feminist Utopian Novels: *Herland*

Nonfiction Classic: *Women and Economics*

JAMAICA
KINCAID

ANTIGUAN-AMERICAN AUTHOR

B. 1949

SORCERESS OF ISLANDS, VENOM, AND HISTORIES

BY DAY, THE island of Antigua sleeps like a white, sandy lion. At night, the lion opens his jaws to swallow young girls whole. When her childhood ends, Jamaica fights her way out of the lion's mouth and swims all the way to America.

JAMAICA PUTS A pot of soup on the stove. It is hearty with hurt, the hurt of nations and families. She leaves the house and goes about her business. By evening, the soup boils down to a thick black sludge. Jamaica scoops it up with her pen and writes.

JAMAICA WALKS HER favorite pet, the Serpent of Language, on a leash: the snake repeats its sinister slither on the sidewalk, edging alongside her mistress and poised to strike.

Jamaica Kincaid was born on Antigua, a former slave-owning British colony in the West Indies. Eager to get away, she moved to the United States at eighteen to work as an au pair. Soon after, she began writing *New Yorker* articles and her intense, biting fiction and nonfiction, which speaks with tremendous authority and clarity and often repeats images and phrases in an insistent invective against the failures of mothers, fathers, siblings, and colonialism.

RECOMMENDED READING

Unforgettable Short Stories: *At the Bottom of the River* (start with "Girl")

Classic Coming-of-Age Novels: *Annie John, Lucy, The Autobiography of My Mother*

Scathing Critique of Caribbean Tourism: *A Small Place*

ANNE CARSON

CANADIAN POET AND CLASSICIST

B. 1950

HIGH PRIESTESS OF SCHOLARS, VOLCANOES, AND EROS

ANNE'S BRAIN, A grim jewel of astronomical price, has been known to exist in several places at once. Its sharp teeth could find your ankle at any moment. Watch out.

SAPPHO, SOKRATES, AND Sophokles are a few of the ghosts that haunt Anne's nights. They follow her from room to room, monologuing in ancient Greek about their pains and losses. Dawn hardens the ghosts into marble. Anne fondles their muscles over coffee and toast.

ANNE OBSERVES A squirrel from her window. Wonders, *What do squirrels know that I don't?* Later, after feasting on the squirrel's eyes, she gains the knowledge she craved. And the squirrel, otherwise left intact, becomes the Blind Shaman of Squirrels, blessed as he's been by the Priestess.

The combination of this MacArthur "Genius" Grant recipient's austerity, startling insights, and relentless questioning is as awe-inspiring and explosive as the volcanoes she has been known to paint. Anne Carson's prolific output of poems, essays, and various hybrids deals with lost family members, love and lust, religion, and the intellectual tradition. She is also a scholar of ancient Greek and Latin texts and a champion of fellow Witches, having translated Sappho and written about Emily Brontë and Virginia Woolf.

RECOMMENDED READING

Our Favorite Poetry and Essays: *Glass, Irony, and God*

Verse Novel Based on a Greek Myth: *Autobiography of Red*

Imaginative Essays on Love: *Eros the Bittersweet*

Most Inventive Sophokles Translation: *Antigonick*

LESLIE MARMON SILKO

LAGUNA PUEBLO NOVELIST

B. 1948

STORYTELLER OF RATTLESNAKES, TURQUOISE, AND THE SACRED DESERT

THE DROUGHT HAS gone on too long, so Leslie tries something new. She roams the arroyos in a mountain lion's shape, talking to the sky. The next morning, rain fills the pawprints in Leslie's yard.

AN ENORMOUS SNAKE coils around Leslie's house, its head guarding the door. It has markings of every color—the colors of every people on Earth, every rock, animal, and plant.

LESLIE TELLS A story, and the story remembers itself. The spider's silk holding all things together shines with the light of Leslie's voice.

Of Pueblo, Mexican, European, and Cherokee ancestry, Leslie Marmon Silko identifies most with the Laguna Pueblo culture, which holds a vital belief in the universe's interconnectedness. Silko's work explores the tensions between the Southwest's diverse communities and methods of healing. Her breakout novel, *Ceremony*—about a young half-Pueblo, half-white man trying to recover from his service in WWII—attracted a major spotlight to Native American literature.

RECOMMENDED READING

Groundbreaking Classic: *Ceremony*

Sprawling Epic: *Almanac of the Dead*

Pueblo Folklore–Inspired Poems and Tales: *Storyteller*

ALEJANDRA PIZARNIK

MINIMALIST ARGENTINE POET

1936-1972

FANTASMA OF SILENCE, DEATH, AND LILACS

A BIRD OF blue bones drops a piece of paper into your hand. The paper unfolds into a palace. You step in through the door. A cold wind blows through the hall, and you hear faint music. Each chord sounds a different note of silence. You keep going.

AT THE END of the hall, you see a paper woman playing a paper harp. Alejandra's eyes are faintly drawn circles, nothing in them. She looks so lonely as her fingers run over the strings. The music hollows. You realize that if you don't leave now, you, too, will turn into a paper doll.

YOU ESCAPE THROUGH the paper door. But there's something in your hand. It's the bird, blue bones turned to paper, singing Alejandra's song. You're cursed to hear it forever. You give in, eat the bird whole. Every once in a while, that lilac song of absence plays across your own ribs.

Born to Russian Jewish parents in Argentina, Alejandra Pizarnik was educated in both Yiddish and Spanish but wrote in Spanish. Her poetry of imagistic purity and surrealist influence summons themes of silence, absence, madness, and death again and again. Her own struggle with depression led to an intentional overdose of Seconal at the age of thirty-six. Already idolized by Spanish-speaking writers, her genius deserves a global readership.

RECOMMENDED READING

Start Here: "Your Voice," "Party," "The Dream of Death, or the Site of Poetical Bodies"

Collection of Best Work: *Extracting the Stone of Madness: Poems 1962–1972*, trans. Yvette Siegert

Slim Volume: *A Musical Hell*, trans. Yvette Siegert

MIRABAI

HINDU MYSTIC AND DEVOTIONAL LOVE POET

1450?-1547?

DAKINI OF HOLY ECSTASY, THE DARK ONE, AND ANKLE BELLS

MIRA CUTS HER hair off for Krishna. Later, she can feel him braiding the discarded strands back together with intense tenderness. Her scalp burns with his touch.

PUDDLES REMEMBER MIRA'S ankle bells as she wanders through the mountains at night, looking for her lover. They play the music of her longing back to one another until morning. By dawn, the mountains are in love.

POISON BECOMES ASHAMED of itself in Mira's presence. It blushes into a holy elixir, promising to merge Mira with her Dark One. Mira drinks the decanter down to the dregs.

Instead of attending to her royal and wifely duties, princess Mirabai wrote intense, erotic devotional poetry to the god Krishna, whom she thought of as her lover. Mirabai's in-laws loathed her unconventional ways, and she miraculously escaped their poisoning attempts twice. When the in-laws tried to bring her back into the family, Mirabai spent the night at a Krishna temple and disappeared forever. Legend has it that she merged with Krishna's image that night—or continued on her spiritual pilgrimage in disguise.

RECOMMENDED READING

Best Translation: *Mirabai: Ecstatic Poems*, trans. Robert Bly and
Jane Hirshfield

Love Poems: "Mira Is Mad with Love," "In All My Lives," "The Door"

Rebellious Poems: "All I Was Doing Was Breathing," "To My
Brother-in-Law Rana"

ANAÏS NIN

AVANT-GARDE AUTHOR OF FICTION AND MEMOIR

1903-1977

UNDINE OF INTROSPECTION, OPULENT DREAMS, AND VOYAGES

ANAÏS FALLS ASLEEP in her sunken glass ship. As she dreams, her many selves rise from her body. They have dark flowing hair, and eyes blink slowly all over their faces, chests, and arms. Some collect seashells, others chart the sun's movement. Some keep house, make lace, pursue lovers. Another operates a printing press. Before dawn, the selves gather around the sleeping Anaïs, kiss each other's eyelids and mouths, and dive back into the single body like the mermaids they are.

ONE OF THESE mermaids goes to the City of Fathers and never comes back. In this city, father statues stand at every square, and shadow fathers slip around every street corner. The mermaid dotes on the statue of Anaïs's father. She cleans the seaweed off his lapels, scares away the fish that nibble on his marble knuckles, and stares into his blank stone eyes.

ANAÏS WRITES HER diary on the waves. The diary crashes on the rocks, stains the moon, splashes the shoes of transients on the wharf with paragraphs of nerves and experience. The ink of consciousness runs down the mermaids' faces.

Born to Cuban parents, Anaïs Nin—sensitive, magnetic, fashionable—was raised in Europe and New York. As an adult in Paris, she forged a fluid new literature of female consciousness. Much has been made of her erotica, but her chief artistry is in the nonlurid works. Nin's fiction and her masterpiece, a lifelong diary, explore the fractured self, her complicated feelings for her father, psychoanalysis, love, and adventures of all sorts.

RECOMMENDED READING

Hypnotic Novels: *House of Incest; Cities of the Interior*

Intoxicating Stories: *Under a Glass Bell*

Grandest Achievement: Seven-volume *Diary of Anaïs Nin*

GERTRUDE STEIN

AMERICAN EXPATRIATE AND MODERNIST INNOVATOR

1874-1946

MADAME OF ROSES, GEOMETRY, AND REPETITION

GERTRUDE IS A spider, weaving a web of funhouse mirrors. Flies trap themselves by staring at their warped reflections, which repeat, repeat, repeat.

FOR GERTRUDE, EACH word is a hedgehog in a metal cage. Gertrude bangs at the cages with a stick; the noise is deafening. The hedgehogs grow feathers, slink into worms, shrink into dragonflies—anything to get out. Only then is Gertrude satisfied.

YOU CAN STILL catch glimpses of Gertrude in miniature, living on in her salon's paintings. There she is, holding hands with Alice B., hobbling off into the shadow of a Cézanne apple. Skiing down the curvy hip of a Matisse nude, yelling with high-pitched glee.

Gertrude Stein's Paris salon was host to a staggering collection of modern art and famous visitors (Picasso, Hemingway, F. Scott Fitzgerald, and so on). Influenced by the radical painters she supported, Stein set out to create cubism in writing. She stripped her poems of narrative and logic, playing instead with spatial relationships and process. She shared her life with her romantic partner and secretary, Alice B. Toklas.

RECOMMENDED READING

Most Approachable: *The Autobiography of Alice B. Toklas*

Famous Cubist Poems: *Tender Buttons*

Woman-Centered Stories: *Three Lives*

YUMIKO KURAHASHI

JAPANESE SURREALIST

1935-2005

SIBYL OF MASKS, EXTRATERRESTRIAL EGGS, AND TWISTED FANTASIES

TROUBLED BY YOUR dreams, you visit Yumiko for a psychic reading. She holds a crystal ball as you describe your visions. "This," she says, picking up the ball and holding it high over her head, "contains your subconscious." She smashes the crystal ball on the ground. You choke in the pungent fumes.

WHEN THE AIR clears, Yumiko is gone. What remains—glass shards and a black, sticky substance. The inky material shapes itself into three sexy cat women and one alien. They begin to caress one another. The deranged creatures walk towards you, paw you, turn you inky, too. . . .

YOU COME TO at the psychic's table. The room is clean and the crystal ball intact. You notice your reflection across the room: you look just like Yumiko! Her small teeth smile back at you. Your black tail flicks with a pleasure that may or may not be your own.

Yumiko Kurahashi, a badass of experimental fiction from Kochi Prefecture, is almost entirely unknown among English speakers. Influenced by Kafka and French literature, Kurahashi's bizarre stories feature ghosts, flying heads, witch masks, incest, and bestiality. Her work will completely freak you out—and provoke you with its fairy-tale logic and philosophical underbelly.

RECOMMENDED READING

Kurahashi sorely needs more English translations!

Disturbing Tales: *The Woman with the Flying Head and Other Stories*, trans. Atsuko Sakaki

Hard-to-Find Political Satire: *The Adventures of Sumiyakist Q*, trans. Dennis Keene

Dream List for Translation: *Cruel Fairy Tales for Adults*; *Cruel Fairy Tales for Old Folks*

Translated by Yumiko into Japanese: Shel Silverstein's *The Missing Piece* and Antoine de Saint-Exupéry's *Le Petit Prince*

AGATHA CHRISTIE

BEST-SELLING BRITISH CRIME NOVELIST

1890-1976

GRAND DAME OF TRICKERY, MURDER, AND TEATIME

AGATHA INVITES YOU to afternoon tea in her garden maze. When you get there, the butler is dead by the table. "Most unpleasant," says Agatha, biting into a scone. "You must help me solve the case before the police arrive. Imagine the headlines: *Mystery Author Puzzled by Murder on Own Lawn*. And I truly do have no idea." She shakes her head, and a stifled cry issues from somewhere in the maze.

"OH DEAR," EXCLAIMS Agatha. "I suppose you will go see what the fuss is about?" As you enter the maze, the walls shift—hedges rise from nowhere, blocking your path, and shrubs shuffle into new formations. Your head spins. You see a bottle glinting in the grass. You pick it up: the label reads POISON. There's a rumble, and to your great surprise, a small glass train bursts through the hedges.

AGATHA LEANS OUT of the dining compartment, sipping from a teacup. "Goodness, I see you've put your fingerprints all over the evidence!" She tsks. "Well, you've been a great help. That butler was such a bore. The police will be here shortly. Farewell!" Agatha throws you a consolatory apricot biscuit. The train takes a sudden turn for the sky, puffing through the clouds.

Agatha Christie's nearly seventy detective novels made her the most popular novelist in all of history. Taking place in a British aristocracy of luxury trains, handsome estates, and butlers, her books keep the reader guessing about the truth behind their murders until the shocking twists are revealed.

RECOMMENDED READING

Biggest Twist: *The Murder of Roger Ackroyd*

Starring Famous Detective #1, Hercule Poirot: *Murder on the Orient Express*

Starring Famous Detective #2, Miss Marple: *A Murder Is Announced*

JANET FRAME

IDIOSYNCRATIC NEW ZEALAND NOVELIST

1924-2004

HERMIT OF HOSPITALS, BELONGING, AND LOST SOULS

A LAGOON FORMS around Janet's every step. Her drowned sisters call out from the water at her feet. Janet puts on her earmuffs to block out the voices.

JANET KEEPS AN eel in a box next to her typewriter. When the eel shakes its box, Janet scolds it: "You think you're the only one who doesn't belong?" And she shows her bad teeth wickedly. Later, repenting, Janet releases the eel back into its native waters. At least some creatures can find a home.

ON SPECIAL NIGHTS, Janet turns out the lights and sits very still until her red hair flames with bright fire. Then the fairies gather around the flame and settle into Janet's curls. They pick through with tenderness, snacking on the crumbs and insects, and Janet beams with a rare happiness.

Janet Frame was born to a large, poor family on a New Zealand farm. Her brother had epilepsy, and two of her sisters drowned in adolescence. Misdiagnosed with schizophrenia, Frame spent most of her twenties in psychiatric wards, receiving two hundred electroshock treatments and narrowly escaping a lobotomy. After her release, she pursued a solitary life, even wearing earmuffs in the privacy of her own home to block out sound, and writing autobiographical fiction about hospitalization and the displaced self.

RECOMMENDED READING

Lovely Stories and Essays: *The Lagoon and Other Stories*

Stream-of-Consciousness Novel on Hospitalization: *Owls Do Cry*

Three-Part Memoir: *To the Is-Land; An Angel at My Table; The Envoy from Mirror City*; adapted into a marvelous film by Jane Campion, *An Angel at My Table*

MARÍA SABINA

MAZATEC HEALER AND ORAL POET

1894-1985

SHAMAN OF DEW, HUMMINGBIRDS, AND MUSHROOM LANGUAGE

IN HER NIGHTIME vigils, María claps and chants with such force that the embroidered eagles fly off her *huipil* and join the gods, beasts, and moonlight whirling around the room.

AS THE MUSHROOMS speak through her, María's bare feet make inscriptions in the great Book of Mud, letters large enough for God to read.

MARÍA RELAXES IN the evenings with the Thunder Lord on the mountain. They share cigarettes and *aguardiente*, and when she's ready to go home, María becomes a star and shoots across the sky.

María Sabina, who could not read or write and lived in poverty in the mountains of southern Mexico, is considered the greatest shaman-poet or Wise One (*chota chijne*) of the Mazatec language. She improvised her chants during psilocybin-mushroom ceremonies, performed to heal the sick. Her rich spiritual vision was informed by native Mazatec beliefs as well as the Catholic faith.

RECOMMENDED READING

Life Story, Chants, and Context: *María Sabina: Selected Works*
   (Poets for the Millennium), ed. by Jerome Rothenberg

MARY SHELLEY

BRITISH AUTHOR OF *FRANKENSTEIN*

1797–1851

ALCHYMIST OF MONSTERS, CHILDREN, THE LIVING AND THE DEAD

AFTER SHE LOSES most of her family, Mary experiments with potions to bring back the departed. She places her mother's papers, locks of her children's hair, and a tiny model of her husband's sailboat into a vial. Pours in seawater, buds from the garden. Shakes.

MARY IS A terrible baby, her very arrival a murder. Frankenstein's Creature is a terrible baby, a torment to his creator. Mary's babies die terribly young. Latest finding from Mary's laboratory: even the freshest thing is mixed with rot.

AT NIGHT, NO matter what she does, Mary's laboratory becomes a cemetery. Lantern becomes moon, instruments become shovels, tables turn to coffins. Mary sighs. She places her hand into the enormous, awkward paw of the waiting Creature, and they walk together among the graves.

Frankenstein isn't the garish zombie story we've seen in pop culture. Inspired by scientific discussions of the day and Shelley's complex feelings about parenting, *Frankenstein* is a painful tale about the creation of life and what happens to shunned, abandoned children. Her life was as harrowing as her famous novel: her great losses of mother (feminist Mary Wollstonecraft died during Shelley's birth), husband (poet Percy Bysshe Shelley drowned in a sailing accident), and children (only one of four survived) tried her ideals of domestic harmony.

RECOMMENDED READING

Revisit This Classic: *Frankenstein: or, The Modern Prometheus*

Gothic Short Story: "The Mortal Immortal"

Neglected Gem: *The Last Man*

ZORA NEALE HURSTON

HARLEM RENAISSANCE STAR, FOLKLORIST,

ANTHROPOLOGIST

1891–1960

CONJURER OF HURRICANES, ZOMBIES, AND TALL TALES

ZORA, KINDLY CRONE, steps up to a country house with an empty basket. Offered something to eat, she asks instead for a story. With each story, she explains, my basket gains an apple. Soon the whole town is on the porch, telling stories and laughing. Zora's basket abounds with apples. She wanders off into the night with her heavy, shining fruit.

BEFORE WRITING, ZORA wills herself into a trance. She wraps a flood around her shoulders like a shawl. The flood whirls with puffer fish, human bones, thunder, and lightning. A crazed dog rises from the water and bites her affectionately on the neck, and then her hand lowers to the page with the gravity of the undead.

ZORA DEDICATES HER final years to ensuring that, at any given minute somewhere in the galaxy, a young woman will climb under a pear tree and contemplate the wonder of her body. So what if Zora must give up writing to make mental room for her planetary efforts? So what if Zora is poor, forgotten, and alone? All the more time to manipulate the cosmos.

When she wasn't writing lush fiction about black women owning themselves, Hurston was collecting folktales around the South and journeying to the Caribbean. There, she initiated into Vodou, once by boiling a live black cat and passing its bones over her lips, and took the first known photograph of a zombie. Hurston fell into obscurity even before her death (she was buried in an unmarked grave) but has seen a major revival of interest in recent decades among readers, feminists, and critics as a key figure in the Harlem Renaissance.

RECOMMENDED READING

Classic Novel: *Their Eyes Were Watching God*

Southern Folklore and Vodou Accounts: *Mules and Men; Tell My Horse*

Controversial Autobiography: *Dust Tracks on a Road*

ACKNOWLEDGMENTS

WE WISH TO THANK Kelly Luce of Electric Literature for taking to the original "Literary Witches" piece and J. Robert Lennon for publishing the piece in Okey-Panky. Huge thanks to our agent, Adriann Ranta Zurhellen, for finding us and believing in this book, and to the publishing team, especially Stephanie Knapp and Alex Camlin, for realizing our visions.

We're also deeply grateful to everyone who debated witchy merits with us and pointed us in the direction of a worthy Witch. Last but not least, we wish to thank our families for their support during the making of this book. We could not have done it without you.

TAISIA KITAISKAIA is the author of *Ask Baba Yaga: Otherworldly Advice for Everyday Troubles*, based on her column voiced by a Slavic witch in The Hairpin. She holds an MFA from the James A. Michener Center for Writers and has published poetry in journals such as *Crazyhorse*, *Guernica*, *Gulf Coast*, *Pleiades*, and *The Fairy Tale Review*.

KATY HORAN channels the Witch archetype through her drawings and paintings of Appalachian granny witches, full moon ceremonies, and strange folk magic. Her work has been shown in galleries throughout North America and featured in anthologies such as *Beasts!* (Fantagraphics), *The Exquisite Book* (Chronicle), and *Dark Inspiration* (Victionary).